DEALI[

MW01610652

CRISIS

Roots of Youth Ministry Series

This series addresses ecumenical and uniquely Presbyterian youth ministry concerns. Volumes in this series are intended for both professional and lay adults engaged in youth ministry.

Series Writers
Rodger Nishioka
Bob Tuttle
Lynn Turnage

Series Editor
Faye Burdick

Titles In Series
The Roots of Who We Are
Surveying the Land
Dealing with Crisis
Rooted in Love
Sowing the Seeds
Growing Leaders
Growing a Group

DEALING WITH
CRISIS

BOB TUTTLE

Bridge Resources
Louisville, Kentucky

Scripture quotations in this publication are from the New Revised Standard Version of the Bible, copyright 1989 by the Division of Christian Education of the National Council of the Churches of Christ in the United States of America. In some instances, the text is slightly altered in the interest of inclusive language. Used by permission.

Every effort has been made to trace copyrights on the materials included in this book. If any copyrighted material has nevertheless been included without permission and due acknowledgment, proper credit will be inserted in future printings after notice has been received.

Edited by Faye Burdick

Book interior and cover design by Pamela Ullman

First edition

Published by Bridge Resources
Louisville, Kentucky

Website address: http://www.pcusa.org/pcusa/currpub

PRINTED IN THE UNITED STATES OF AMERICA

97 98 99 00 01 02 03 04 05 06 — 10 9 8 7 6 5 4 3 2 1

Library of Congress Catalog-in-Publication Data

Tuttle, Bob, 1949–
    Dealing with crisis / Bob Tuttle. — 1st ed.
        p.   cm. — (Roots of youth ministry series)
    Includes bibliographical references.
    ISBN 1-57895-009-0
    1. Church work with teenagers. 2. Teenagers — Pastoral counseling of.
    3. Teenagers—United States. I. Title. II. Series.
    BV447.T88 1997
        259'.23—dc21.   97–10159

Contents

Acknowledgments

This book was a tough one to write, not only because of the content, but also because I, and my family, have lived through some of it. I have been convinced for a number of years that adult leaders needed a basic resource in dealing with crises with young people and that this resource would need to be simple enough so as not to be overwhelming. The risk, of course, was that it would not be comprehensive enough to satisfy those well experienced with particular issues. Rodger Nishioka and Lynn Turnage encouraged me to take up my own challenge, and I'm grateful to them. All three of us are especially grateful to Flora and Rick Hobson and their sons David, Patrick, and Cauley for their gracious hospitality.

I want to thank my wife, Pat, my son, Chris, and my daughter, Sarah, for their love and encouragement. Chris (under the great leadership of teacher Barbara Epley) and Sarah have had the advantage of being participants in a "Peer Helping" program at Owen High School in Swannanoa, North Carolina. The resources that Chris brought home from this program started me thinking about the possibility of doing something akin to such a program within the church. I want to express my gratitude to Mama and Diane for always believing in me. I acknowledge the wisdom that I have gained from all of the colleagues, both paid and volunteer, that I have had the privilege of ministering with over these many years. And lastly, I want to recognize the support and guidance that I have received from the Program Office at Montreat Conference Center over the last ten years, most especially Sandy Jividen. Thanks for being my friends.

To the readers: This book is only a beginning for me, and I hope for you.

Survivors of a Completed Suicide

Scene One

The call from the pastor of the church where I was director of Christian education came at breakfast. He had decided not to call me in the middle of the night because there was not much anyone could have done. He had spent the night by the bedside of a junior high in our church whose head had been wrapped in bloody towels. There had been no need to "pull the plug." Everyone knew that the bullet he had put through his brain would mean that he would not live through the night.

He had taken out the trash like a good little boy and then took his bicycle and disappeared. After a long frantic search, they had found him with one other household item that they had not discovered missing until that moment—a family revolver that had been hidden in the top of the closet. He had blown his brains out, alone in the cold and dark. I don't remember much about suicide notes except that he did leave more than one in his room. I do remember visiting the boy's parents and having a very awkward conversation. He was not well known by the youth at church and his parents were not active members. It later made perfect sense that they seemed a little angry at all of the sudden attention. "Why," they seemed to say, "didn't people come around and visit and express their concern *before* he killed himself?"

Scene Two

I was away at a summer conference with colleagues and members of a family in our congregation. A grandmother was with us, and her granddaughter was babysitting our young son. We were all staying in a rental cottage together. The phone rang. I was summoned upstairs by our associate pastor—I had to help him break the tragic news to the two women that their grandson and brother had killed himself. Even more tragically, he had planned his death so that his mother would come home from work and find his body. This young adult, for reasons unknown to me then and now, had barricaded himself with his little outdoor charcoal cooker in their bathroom, sealed all the cracks with towels, made himself a comfortable pillow, and laid down to a sleep made forever by carbon monoxide poisoning.

Overview of a Completed Suicide

First, a note about language. Although the experiences above labeled the young men as two who "killed themselves," most statisticians (and many loved ones as well) prefer to describe them as "suicide completers" or "suiciders."

Language of Suicide Completers

The term "suicide completer" has a number of advantages.

- It is a good substitute for "committed suicide." This avoids either the criminal connotation of having "committed" a crime or the image of "being committed" to a mental institution.

- It describes them in terms of having completed something that many, many Americans have admitted thinking about. It makes more obvious the fact that they are different from most of us only because of one action that they took and that we didn't.

- It avoids having to refer to them as having "done something to themselves" when that was not their aim at all.

- It avoids referring to those now dead in a negative, judgmental manner and instead labels them in a more objective manner.

Obviously, though, this is a pastoral issue. If other wording "feels better" to the survivors of completed suiciders, then use the language that *they* prefer.

Although it may seem very odd to note, there is some good news about suicide in this country:

- 99.9 percent of North Americans *don't* kill themselves.

- The overall suicide rate in our country is probably leveling off.

- Talking about suicide does *not* cause someone to be suicidal.

- Suicide is preventable. Most suicide victims do *not* want to die.

With that, of course, comes the *bad news*

- In the United States, thirty thousand people kill themselves each year.[1]

- Suicide is the third-leading killer of fifteen- to twenty-four-year-olds (behind accidents and alcohol-related deaths).[2]
- The suicide rate for adolescents is up more than 200 percent over the past four decades.[3]

And then there are the just plain facts

- Three to four times as many men as women complete suicide.[4]
- It is a myth that suicide is usually due to mental illness, although persons suffering from mental illness do have much higher suicide rates.[5]
- 1994 statistics for the United States indicate that 318 ten- to fourteen-year-olds completed suicide.[6] Extrapolating from this data, and assuming (rightly or wrongly) that the number has remained the same, one middle schooler will complete suicide every twenty-eight hours this year in the United States.
- 1994 statistics indicate that 1948 fifteen- to nineteen-year-olds completed suicide in the United States.[7] Extrapolating from this data, and assuming (rightly or wrongly) that the number has remained the same, one senior high will complete suicide every 4.5 hours this year in the United States.

Although we run a great risk in trying to describe anyone as "typical" in these cases, it seems worthwhile to draw from various sources some characteristics.

Typical Adolescent Suicide Completer

The typical adolescent suicide completer

- was male (three times more males complete suicide than females)[8]
- was a younger person in the family
- tried to solve problems on his own
- may have used alcohol or drugs as a way to solve problems
- found it difficult to seek outside help, especially from adults
- did not confide in friends
- tried to please parents
- tried to be what parents wanted him or her to be
- found little recognition for what he or she really was

- consumed a large amount of alcohol during final few hours
- had a major confrontation with a meaningful person during the last twenty-four hours
- made desperate attempts to contact a friend(s) by phone

Before we begin to think about how we help our young people deal with the impact on the peers, friends, and family members of a completed suicide, it might also be helpful to note the mindset of the suicider. From suicide notes and conversations that the deceased had with friends or relatives, most researchers draw the conclusion that the primary emotion of the suicider is *helplessness*. They are unable to escape the dilemma they find themselves in and they feel a complete loss of control. These are some of the feelings they experience:

> can't stop the pain
> can't think clearly
> can't make decisions
> can't see any way out
> can't sleep, eat, or work
> can't get out of depression
> can't make the sadness go away
> can't see a future without pain
> can't see themselves as worthwhile
> can't get someone's attention
> can't seem to get control

Why do they do it? The answers are numerous, but once again comments made or notes left give us a variety of motives:

- Revenge, especially in an already passive-aggressive person, is suspected when it is obvious that specific others were intended to be spectators. One message is "I'm not very happy." The other message is "It's your fault."
- Romance in a "Romeo and Juliet" style is often a motive, both in single and couple completed suicides. Notes may even say "I can't go on living without (name)."
- Dreams of immortality figure in other completed suicides. "I'm

escaping from the realm of reality into the darkness of the unknown . . ." is a typical quote of those for whom death is a vague notion, a magical, mystical place.

- Many think that "suicide is painless." A long, peaceful sleep will somehow make things better.

- The "I want it now" mentality noted in all of us these days is especially dangerous in the territory of adolescence. It's hard for the young person to understand that three months from now (much less three years) is a short time in the whole span of life.

- There is emerging research now supporting the suspicion that the struggle to establish sexual orientation and the affirmation of sexual orientation may play a role in the decision to complete suicide.

In the same way that it was helpful to note the mindset of the suicider, so it might also be helpful to profile the emotions of *survivors*.

- Their grief is deep at this sudden death.

- They often feel guilty at not having done enough to stop the suicider.

- They might be angry at the suicider for "leaving" them.

- They may indeed feel some of the same pain and helplessness that the suicider felt.

- They may feel shame at the stigma that our society typically places on suiciders as being too "weak" to stand up to the stress of everyday life.

- They often feel isolated because their friends are uncomfortable talking about suicide.

- They often blame themselves for what happened.

- They are shocked at the suddenness of the act and its result.

- If the facts of the death are not completely clear, they may deny that it was a suicide. If the fact of the suicide itself is undeniable, they may deny that there was any reason for the suicide.

A final word before we launch into our program design to be offered to the young people: There may be some in your congregation who will be afraid that just *talking* about suicide with the young people in your congregation is dangerous, that it might in some way *encourage* suicide. No research can substantiate this view. In fact, research points in the opposite direction:

- There can never be too much communication between young

people and the adults who care for and with them.

- Building skills for coping with life's crises among young people is valuable for their own self-esteem and self-worth.

- Building skills for coping with life's crises among young people can help save the lives of other youth people.

Program Design for Learning How to Help Friends Who Are Survivors of a Completed Suicide

Theme

You *can* make a difference.

Objectives

Participants will be able to

- use nonjudgmental language in describing suicide situations

- profile the "typical" suicide completer

- list five reasons why families of suicide completers might feel isolated

- list five actions they can take to reach out to those families

Materials Needed

- Index cards

- Copies of "Profile of a Typical Suicide Completer"

- Pencils/pens

➤➤ Activity One ◀◀

Photocopy and hand out the following quiz, "Profile of a Typical Suicide Completer." Provide time for participants to complete responses.

➤➤ Activity Two ◀◀

Gather the group together and share responses to the quiz. Current data offers these answers: (1) male; (2) three times; (3) younger; (4) on their own; (5) yes; (6) no; (7) yes; (8) no; (9) tried to contact friends. Use the language of the quiz itself to raise the issue of why we use different terms than "kill themselves." Make some quick comments about language using the paragraph from page 2 this chapter.

Profile of a Typical Suicide Completer

1. The typical suicide completer is: (choose one)

    ❏ male   ❏ female

2. How many more of the gender chosen above complete suicide than the other gender?

    ❏ twice   ❏ three times   ❏ four times

3. Is the typical suicide completer a younger or older person in their family?

    ❏ younger   ❏ older

4. Do they try to solve problems with the help of others or own their own?

    ❏ with help of others   ❏ on their own

5. Do they find it difficult to seek outside help, especially from adults?

    ❏ yes   ❏ no

6. Are they usually able to confide in more than one friend?

    ❏ yes   ❏ no

7. Have they usually had a major confrontation with a meaningful person during the last twenty-four hours?

    ❏ yes   ❏ no

8. Have they usually had lots of recognition for the person that they really were?

    ❏ yes   ❏ no

9. Have they usually kept their last struggles over whether to live or die to themselves or have they usually tried to contact friends?

    ❏ kept to themselves   ❏ tried to contact friends

➤➤ Activity Three ◀◀

Break into five different groups (for small groups, divide index cards between two different groups), each with an index card or piece of paper with one of these phrases written on it:

- the shock of sudden death

- denial that the person completed suicide

- anger at the person for leaving

- confusion over why the person completed suicide

- embarrassment that their loved one completed suicide

Give each group ten minutes to come up with a sample conversation that explains their index card with someone who has come to visit them. Encourage participants to start off by saying, "I'm. . . ."

➤➤ Activity Four ◀◀

Role-play these conversations in front of the whole group. Cut them off before they start winding down. It's always better to leave them begging for more.

➤➤ Activity Five ◀◀

Debrief the exercise and end by pointing out that Christ promises to always be with us *(Matthew 28:20b)*.

By looking at Christ in Scripture we can gain a better understanding of how our faith should undergird all that we are in life and all that we do to support suffering survivors of completed suicide. They can be assured that Jesus was very understanding toward people with personal problems like those of their loved one. He understood that people had difficulty with decisions and sometimes made poor ones. He offered acceptance to those heavily burdened: "Come to me, all you that are weary and are carrying heavy burdens, and I will give you rest" *(Matthew 11:28)*. Jesus suffered in many ways just like us and felt like even God had forsaken him *(Matthew 27:46)*. Close with prayer giving thanks for the gifts of life, forgiveness, and grace.

Help for the Adult Leader

Here are many ways you can help survivors of the suicide completer.

- Make an extra-special effort to go to the funeral home. The shock, denial, and embarrassment are overwhelming for survivors. They need all the support they can get.

- When the survivor is receiving friends, act as you would at any funeral and offer them a hug. It's OK to say, "I'm so very sorry."

- Suicide survivors may be more sensitive and embarrassed than normal. An extra card or visit from you in the next few weeks may really help.

- If you hear others making vicious or cruel remarks, stop them, and by all means don't repeat the remarks. Help the person spreading these remarks to understand how much they can hurt the survivors.

- Write the date of death on your calendar one year from now so that you can call, visit, or write a note. The anniversary of a suicide is a very painful time.

- For an adolescent survivor of a suicide, it might be appropriate to follow up even sooner. Why not mark your calendar for a three, six, and nine-month anniversary as well?

There are also many things that you may hear other well-meaning people saying, but that you should *avoid*.

- Don't try to comfort them with weak explanations, such as "They didn't know what they were doing," or "They were drunk or on drugs," or "It was an accident." How do you know? You weren't there.

- Don't tell the survivor that "God needed" their loved one. Suicide is a human act, done for human reasons, attempted and completed by human beings.

- Don't say that the survivor was "mentally ill" or "crazy." This may raise unnecessary fear in the mind of the survivor about their own mental health or the mental health of other family members.

- Don't relate stories (even if true) of someone you knew and loved who almost committed suicide. Your loved one is alive and theirs isn't.

- Don't try to help the survivor understand "why?" Suicide is usually caused by a number of factors over a period of years with no single explanation. Most likely the victim was not even fully aware of why they were choosing suicide, so how could the survivors ever be clear about the matter? They just need help in living *without* an answer.

- Don't tell them not to be angry with God. This is natural, and it does the survivor no good to keep their anger smoldering inside. If we have anger with God we might as well admit it. God is aware of it anyway.

Loss and grief are a natural part of life. A person in grief may experience a wide variety of strong emotions, some more than others: numbness, denial, anger, shock, depression, confusion, guilt, fear. Grief has a beginning, a middle, and perhaps for a limited few an end. There are no time limits. The task of any caring person, whether an adult leader or a young person, whether friend, relative, or acquaintance, is to assist the bereaved in moving through those natural emotional stages and to encourage them to grow at the same time.

Healthy Survivors

At the end (if there ever is an end) or lessening of the bereavement process, healthy survivors have an opportunity to emerge with

- a renewed sense of personal growth

- the knowledge that they have weathered the storm and are stronger for it

- the awareness of specific sources of support around them in a time of crisis

- a greater capacity for empathy with others facing the struggles of life

- a greater appreciation for other persons around them and for the value of life itself

- a stronger and more resilient faith in God

Attempted Suicide

What's the Problem?

An estimated ten percent of high school students have attempted suicide at one time or another. Other reports put it another way: There are estimates that for every person who completes suicide, there are twenty who attempt it.[1] Statistics and facts are certainly one of the great problems in getting a handle on attempted suicide.

If we are to work with those who have attempted suicide or to answer the concerns of a young person who has a friend who has attempted suicide, it makes sense for us to spend some time considering why the suicide rate has risen so dramatically. We may find some ways to be of help by examining two societal issues before we turn to more personal issues.

There are those who would agree with Raymond Lawrence in his essay in *The Christian Century* that in our world today, life is so cheap that some individuals can't help but draw the erroneous conclusion that their own life is also cheap.

There are others who believe that suicide (as well as other maladies of our society) is an unintended consequence of our higher quality of life.

Suicide among "gifted" adolescents seems to be a special population segment that is worth paying attention to as we discuss suicide attempts and prevention strategies. With a 250 percent increase in suicide among young people since 1964,[2] it seems that gifted young people are especially at risk with the pressure that they place on themselves. Expectations of family members and peers and adults at school and church raise the stakes higher. More research is needed in this area, though. Whether it can be proved or not, there are many who see gifted adolescents as those referred to by Hermann Hesse in the now famous *Steppenwolf* (New York: Bantam Books, 1975, p. 55): "Just as those who at the least indisposition develop a fever, so do those we call suicides. . . . who are always very emotional and sensitive, [and who] develop at the least shock the notion of suicide. . . ."[3]

Although we run a great risk in trying to describe anyone as "typical" in these cases, it seems worthwhile to draw from various sources some characteristics.

Typical Adolescent Suicide Attempter

- is female (90 percent)

- is a firstborn child

- may be very close to her mother

- may depend on her mother for her self-esteem

- may fear separation from her mother

- may have difficulty expressing anger

- may be very nurturing. They are often known for being able to give help to others

- may have an absent father (either absent physically from the home or psychologically unavailable)

- may believe that she has caused a divorce or separation (if there is one in the family)

- may feel abandoned

- may devote too much time and energy to a boyfriend

- may feel depressed, unloved, and unlovable when that boyfriend breaks up with her

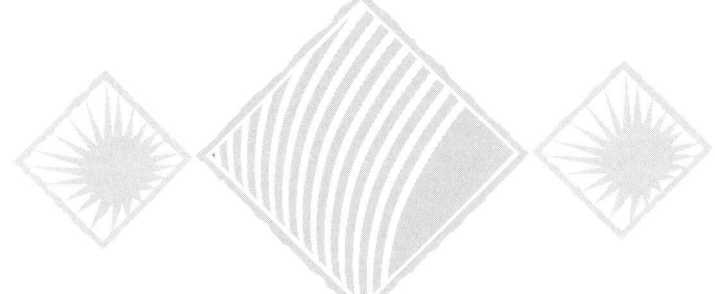

Program Design for Learning about Suicide Attempts

Theme

Suicide can be prevented—and you can help!

Objectives

By the end of the session the participants will be able to

- recognize four feelings that persons considering suicide may have
- role-play a conversation with someone considering suicide
- name five persons that they can turn to in time of trouble

Materials Needed

- Paper
- Crayons
- Index cards
- Phone book or church directory
- Copies of "What to Do" and "What Not to Do," p. 14.

➤➤➤ Activity One ◄◄◄

Have drawing paper and crayons available. Before the activity begins, write each of the feelings from the previous chapter that someone considering suicide might have on index cards, one to a card: (1) shock of sudden death; (2) denial that the person completed suicide; (3) anger at the person for leaving; (4) confusion over why the person completed suicide; (5) embarrassment that their loved one completed suicide. As the group comes in, ask them to pick a card and draw a picture to illustrate this feeling. Tell participants to be prepared to show it to the group.

➤➤➤ Activity Two ◄◄◄

Divide the group in half. Give a copy of "What to Do" to one group, and a copy of "What Not to Do" to the other group. Have the first group role-play demonstrations of what *to* do and the second group role-play demonstrations of what *not* to do.

What to Do

Learn what to do! Be aware of the feelings the person considering suicide has. The person who decided not to attempt suicide is one who either realized on their own or with the help of others that the crisis is temporary and that death is not.

- Take all suicide threats seriously.
- Talk to the person and get help immediately.
- If you suspect that they are considering suicide, ask them, "Are you thinking of hurting yourself?"
- Be willing to listen and allow the person to express their feelings without you expressing your judgment.
- Point the person toward sources of help for problems.
- Let the young person know of their worth as a person, of what they mean to you, and of their worth as a child of God.
- If you consider the suicide imminent, get a verbal contract from them that they will not do anything to hurt themselves until you can get help to them. If it is safe, provide someone to stay with them until you can locate help.
- Assure the suicidal person that they are important.
- If the person thinks that no one will miss them, assure them that their death will have a negative impact on many of their friends and family.
- If you know that the person possesses the means to complete suicide and you can remove those means without getting hurt yourself, do so.

What Not to Do

What not to do when someone close to you is considering suicide.

- Don't dare the person to do it.
- Don't tell the person that they are only joking.
- Don't give assurances that "things will be all right" if you don't really know that.
- Don't ask the person why they are considering suicide. Just listen and they'll tell you.
- Don't offer sympathy ("poor baby"), but offer understanding and hope for the future.
- Don't act shocked.
- Don't lecture the person.
- Don't be sworn to secrecy.

Dealing with Crisis

What Can the Church Do?

After the role play, share with youth what Joyce Ann Mercer says in the August 1996 *Alert* magazine the church can do.[4]

- Offer the young people opportunities to interact with other caring adults.

- Involve the young people in mission to help them gain perspective on their own problems.

- A strong family offers support to a young person and makes them feel better about themselves. Offer opportunities to support families of all kinds, shapes, and sizes in your church's program.

- Act as a community of hope and strength when tragedy does strike. Demonstrate to those still living that God's love, not death, has the final word.

▶▶▶ Activity Three ◀◀◀

Hand out an index card and pencil to each participant. Have a phone book and/or church directory handy as a reference. Give these instructions to the group.

- Take a few moments now to consider this question. If you really needed to talk to someone who could help you think through a particularly troubling issue, who would you call or visit? Try to think of two to three people your own age as well as two to three adults. Use the church directory and phone book to write down their name, home address, and phone number.

After time has been given to fill in the card, the adult leader should ask the young people to choose one other person with whom they should share what they wrote on the card. Close the activity and this program design with the following challenge:

- If you don't have five names, or are missing a young person or adult name, think harder and add to the card during this coming week.

- Keep the card handy (in your backpack, wallet, or purse) so you can have it available for someone in trouble.

Assure youth that people are waiting and willing to listen to them, to help them, and to talk to them. There is always hope and help! Close with prayer giving thanks for people who listen and care.

Help for the Adult Leader

Although there is great debate over this issue, after a completed suicide there is more and more concern about other young people and the possibility of "cluster suicides." Will a completed suicide encourage a young person who might have been thinking about suicide? Will a completed suicide encourage a young person who has already attempted suicide once to attempt it again? Although it seems harsh to some, there seems to be a growing consensus that elements that might seem to naturally flow after any other death of a young person should be removed following a completed suicide.

- Many schools are refusing to lower their flags to half-mast in an effort to avoid any symbolism of a hero's death.

- A principal at one school meeting, instead of offering a eulogy or prayer, asked the audience to "take a moment to silently reflect on today's tragedy and to consider the alternatives [he] might have chosen."[5]

- Mementos, notes, and flowers are often left at the scene of a tragedy or memorial. We have seen these on the fence around the Oklahoma City bomb site and at the Vietnam memorial wall. Suggestions are being made that in the case of completed suicides, these memorials should be removed daily and taken to the family.

Learn the warning signs! A suicidal person may talk about committing suicide, have trouble eating or sleeping, or withdraw from friends and social activities. Watch for drastic changes in behavior. They may lose interest in hobbies, work, and school. They may prepare for death by making out a will. They may try to give away prized possessions. They may take unnecessary risks. They may have had a recent severe loss. They may appear preoccupied with death and dying. They may lose interest in their personal appearance. They may increase their use of drugs and alcohol. These are signs that cannot be ignored.

3

Alcohol Abuse

Scene One

The pastor approached me asking for both advice and encouragement. She had been hearing rumors for months that one of the young people in the church's youth group had been drinking. This concerned her not only because it was illegal in that state but also because of the other impacts alcohol use and potential abuse had on a young person and their family. Many of the warning signs were appearing: Old friendships within the church were dying, and new acquaintances were being made outside of the church who were known to be the "party crowd." His attendance at church activities was becoming sporadic. His grades were slipping. His physical appearance was deteriorating.

The pastor was determined to confront him and make his family aware of the problem as well. My instincts told me that this was a right time for intervention. The pastor confronted him in private and he admitted he was drinking. They agreed to set a time to meet with his parents where he would admit his problem to them in the pastor's presence. The pastor arranged to "drop by for a visit" at the appointed time and spent a very anxious few minutes with the parents because the young person was not there. But he finally arrived, shared the news of his situation, and, after shock and tears, agreed to begin counseling.

Scene Two

They had signed a covenant saying that they wouldn't use alcohol, but it obviously hadn't meant anything to them. We were on a presbytery junior high retreat and noticed on the very first evening of the program that six of the young people were missing. It didn't take long to discover why. A couple of them had absconded with a number of small airline liquor bottles that their parents had collected. Although none were really drunk, they had been passing the bottles around, even on the bus ride to the camp. We packed up the violators and drove them home, arriving so early in the morning on Saturday that we told them to camp out in the church school room until a reasonable hour. Then we would call their parents. Seven A.M. rolled around and we made the phone calls.

Just the Facts

- In 1993, an estimated 17,461 persons were killed in alcohol-related crashes. These deaths accounted for 43.5 percent of 40,115 total traffic fatalities.[1]

- It is estimated that 950,000 people were injured in 1993 in crashes where police or medical personnel reported alcohol was present. That is an average of one injury every 33 seconds.[2]

- About 24 percent of fifteen- to twenty-year-old drivers killed in traffic crashes had a blood alcohol content (BAC) of .10 or higher.[3]

- Direct costs of alcohol-related crashes are estimated to be forty-four billion dollars yearly, including six billion dollars in direct medical costs. An additional ninety billion dollars is lost in quality of life due to these crashes.[4]

- Following a decrease from 37.3 percent in 1979 to 15.7 percent in 1992, the rate of current alcohol use among youth twelve to seventeen years old has stabilized (18 percent in 1993 and 16.3 percent in 1994).[5]

- In 1995, approximately 111 million persons age twelve and over were current alcohol users, which was about 52 percent of the total population age twelve or older.[6]

- About ten million current drinkers were under age twenty-one in 1995. Of these, 4.4 million were binge drinkers, including 1.7 million heavy drinkers.[7]

- The level of alcohol use was strongly associated with illicit drug use in 1995, as in prior years.[8]

- Young adult drinkers (eighteen to twenty-five years old) were the most likely to binge or drink heavily. About half of the drinkers in this age group were binge drinkers and about one in five were heavy drinkers.[9]

- In contrast to the pattern for illicit drugs, the higher the level of educational attainment, the more likely the current use of alcohol.[10]

- Use of alcohol, a "gateway" drug, usually precedes other drug use. A survey of 27,000 seventh to twelfth graders in New York State found little or no use of other drugs among teens who had not used alcohol first.[11]

- Drivers sixteen to twenty-four years old represent approximately 17 percent of all licensed drivers, but are involved in about 36 percent of all fatal alcohol-related crashes.[12]

- Before turning eighteen years old, the average child will see 75,000 drinking scenes on television programs.[13]

Overview of Alcohol Abuse

Alcoholism tends to run in families. There were an estimated 28.6 million Children of Alcoholics (COAs) in the United States in 1991, nearly seven million of them under age eighteen.[14] COAs are at high risk for alcohol and other drug problems and often have already developed, or are likely to develop in the future, unhealthy living patterns.

When guardians—family members (parents, grandparents, or aunts and uncles) in charge of children—are alcoholic, it is likely that the children in these families will develop the disease of alcoholism as well. Of those under age eighteen, almost three million will develop alcoholism and/or other drug problems.[15] Children living with alcoholics are at an increased risk because of genetic factors and possibly because of environmental factors. Even COAs adopted by nonalcoholics (or who don't live with their alcoholic parents) may have a genetic predisposition to alcoholism. Alcoholism can skip a generation, with a genetic vulnerability even manifesting itself in grandchildren.

Children living with alcoholics often develop unhealthy living patterns. They often live with great stress and tension and do poorly in school. They may experience problems coping and have high levels of anxiety and depression. They are at higher risk for school failure. They may not learn valuable skills often found in healthy families: how to trust others, how to build positive relationships, how to handle uncomfortable feelings. Many do make positive adjustments. We'll spell out ways you as an adult leader can help in these adjustments at the end of this chapter.

Alcoholism is a disease that causes physical and psychological addiction. It is *primary* in that it is not a symptom of another disease. It is *progressive* in that if it is not treated, it will worsen. It is *chronic* in that there is no cure or recovery. Only total abstinence from alcohol will keep it from worsening. On top of that, it is fatal if not treated. It can kill.

The stages of alcohol use and abuse seem to parallel those of most social recreational drug use:

- *Stage 1: Experimentation*—Everyone who ever uses drugs or alcohol starts here and either decides they like the feeling and will try it again sometime or decides for whatever reason that they do not want to try it again.

- *Stage 2: Occasional use*—The drug (alcohol) is used once or twice a month, with the user feeling no great craving for alcohol and no fear of getting into heavier drugs. The transition between stage 2 and stage 3 is the best time to get the person help, but it may be one of the hardest because they are convinced that they can handle themselves.

- *Stage 3: Regular use*—The drug is being used one to four times a week on average with the user exhibiting a noticeable attitude change. They talk more and more about getting high and going to parties just to get drunk. The regular user will still be able to do their schoolwork and keep most people from noticing they have a problem. To really stop drinking they would probably need professional help, perhaps outpatient therapy.

- *Stage 4: Addiction*—The person uses the drug anywhere from five times a week to several times a day. Nothing is important to them anymore except getting a drink. They will become secretive, lie, cheat, or steal to support their habit. Now they couldn't stop if they had to or wanted to stop. To really stop drinking they would probably need much more involved and expensive inpatient therapy.

Alcohol is a central nervous system depressant. The physical path that alcohol takes in the body is well documented. Beer, wine, and hard liquor all contain ethyl alcohol, which first goes to the stomach. Unlike food, it does not need to be broken down by digestive enzymes first. Some is absorbed directly through the walls of the stomach, although most of it is absorbed in the first part of the small intestine. The bloodstream carries alcohol to all parts of the body. The liver breaks down the alcohol carried by the bloodstream into water, carbon dioxide, and sugar. It takes about an hour to break down half an ounce of alcohol (roughly the amount in a can or beer, a glass of wine, or a shot of hard liquor). Alcohol reaches the brain last, but within minutes after it is consumed, and it keeps passing through the brain and the rest of the body until the liver has had time to break down all of the alcohol consumed.

The physical effects of prolonged use of alcohol are also well documented. The heart can become enlarged, leading to heart disease. There can be memory loss and loss of coordination. There can be damage to the liver, the kidney, and the stomach. Alcohol can affect the male ability to reproduce and perform sexually. It can lower the level of testosterone in the body, leading to atrophy of the testicles and impotence. In pregnant women there can be birth defects, mental retardation, miscarriage, or stillbirth. Death can result:

- if the alcoholic is not treated and organs important to life function become severely damaged;

- from the person choking on vomit when they are passed out;
- from a coma caused by a depressed heart and breathing; or from the "gag reflex" caused by chugging alcohol, which closes off the esophagus and results in asphyxiation.

A Program Design on Alcohol Abuse

Theme

Learn to help a friend . . . and stay out of a tight spot yourself.

Objectives

By the end of the session, the participants will be able to

- list five reasons teenagers abuse alcohol
- list three consequences of heavy alcohol use
- role-play what to do and what not to do with a friend who has had too much to drink

Materials Needed

- Bibles
- Bible concordances
- Newsprint and markers
- Tape
- Copies of "Just the Facts," page 18

As You Begin

Unlike some drugs, in most states alcohol use by persons below the age of twenty-one is alcohol abuse. It's against the law and has negative consequences for both the young person, the person who sells or gives them the alcohol, and their family. Nevertheless this program design will focus on the effects of alcohol abuse on others, how you as a friend can help, and ways that might make it easier to say no.

➤➤ Activity One ◄◄

Ask the group to help you build a list of reasons teenagers might try to excuse their use of alcohol. Use a chalkboard or sheet of newsprint and marker to record their responses.

Among them may be
- bored
- lonely
- don't know how much it can hurt them
- nothing else to do
- can't sleep
- see other people drinking
- are always around other people who are drinking
- want to do what others are doing
- don't think it will hurt them
- like the feeling
- don't think it hurts other people
- think its their own business
- like to find out about things for themselves
- keeps them from thinking about unpleasant things
- just curious
- can't say no
- looking for something new to do
- want to change their lives
- think everybody drinks
- feel sorry for themselves
- think nobody cares about them or what they do
- it's cool
- it's risky and adventurous
- it's an escape from problems or stress
- my family drinks, so why shouldn't I?

⟫⟫ Activity Two ⟪⟪

Using the information found in "Just the Facts" on page 18, share some of the consequences of heavy alcohol use.

⟫⟫ Activity Three ⟪⟪

Instead of focusing on heavy drinking, tell the group that you will address a more real situation. Pose the following problem:

You're at a party and your ride home has had too much to drink. *You* know that over one-third of young people killed in alcohol-related accidents *were not drinking*, so you're not about to ride home with them. You also know that caffeine won't sober your friend up. It may make your friend less sleepy, but they'll still be drunk. Only time can sober someone up and improve their ability to make decisions.

Ask participants to get into groups of two or three and think about all of the possible solutions to the situation and be prepared to act the solutions out. Give the groups five to ten minutes to work out a scenario. You may let them go into other rooms and practice or talk so they won't be overheard. Gather them back together and go around the pairs as many times as necessary, role-playing the possible solutions. Talk about strengths in each solution.

➤ Activity Four ◄

Using a concordance, look up instances of the word "drunk" or "drunkenness" in the Bible. Provide time for researching and sharing some of these biblical references. Tell the group that although people drank wine in biblical times and still do in many Middle Eastern countries today, the Bible writers seem to be clear that drunkenness was a state that led to many other sins and was to be avoided. At the same time, people with personal problems were never rejected by Jesus or turned away. They were lovingly listened to, confronted when necessary, and supported by the body of believers. That is what we are called to do even today.

➤ Activity Five ◄

Help youth to think of ways to say no. Work as a group on building refusal skills. Suggest the following responses (and ask them for more ideas to add to this list):

- "No thanks, I don't drink."
- "No, I don't like the taste."
- "No, I don't want to get in trouble."
- "No, I'm in training."
- "No, I've got to drive and want to get home in one piece."
- "No, I've got a test tomorrow and have to study when I get home."
  Close with a prayer asking for wisdom, understanding, and courage.

Help for the Adult Leader

Adult leaders should walk a fine line in the area of alcohol use, depending on your own feelings about the use of alcohol. Probably the most important thing here is to be genuine, to have integrity. Even if the young people don't agree with you, at least perhaps they'll recognize your integrity and respect your refusal to be a hypocrite. Here's what I recommend:

- Adult leaders on church-sponsored activities with young people in their care should not drink. Period. This can either be seen simply as refusing to present a situation that could be misinterpreted or refusing to be a "stumbling block" *(1 Cor. 8:9)* in the way of the young person.

- Adult leaders in public, in private, and not "on duty" as a leader of youth, if choosing to use alcohol, should do so in moderation. Refer to the preceding definitions of social recreational drug use to make sure that *you* are not in a hazardous category.

- Adult leaders should refrain from having conversations with each other in front of young people or with young people themselves about drinking and any pleasure it gives them. They should refrain from wearing articles of clothing or bumper stickers that may be interpreted by the youth as endorsing alcohol use.

- In the privacy of their own home, adult leaders should let their conscience be their guide. But it is hoped that alcohol would not be in an obvious location and in large quantities, so that young people visiting the adult leader would not draw the conclusion that the adult leader is a binge or heavy drinker.

Should abstinence from alcohol use during a church youth event be included in any covenant for that activity? Sure! And adult leaders should sign the covenant as well as youth participants, as a gesture of inclusivity, if nothing else.

Use the two scenes from the beginning of this chapter in a discussion group with other adult leaders to talk about "what ifs." Like so many other situations, there can never be enough conversation between adult leaders regarding what they would do in possible situations. Strive for integrity as well as consistency. Conversation about intervention should always include a church staff person, preferably a pastor or a professional counselor.

Alcoholism is a family illness. Typical problems in a family that includes an adult alcoholic include

- resentment that the alcoholic parent won't do anything about the problem
- financial difficulties, caused by not only the cost of buying alcohol but by the loss of job security
- aggressive behavior by other members of the family who have so much stress that they act out in situations with others
- guilt by everyone involved that they may have caused the alcoholic to drink
- helplessness by everyone involved that they can't help the alcoholic get over their problems
- emotional withdrawal from the commitment of all family members to the family itself or to each other
- shame felt by all family members, especially when they try to hide or deny the problem

What happens when a young person in an alcoholic home asks you for help? Sometimes helping a COA means directing them to someone with special skills, but for you as their adult leader, being there for them and listening with compassion is often the real beginning in help. Encourage them to share their thoughts and feelings. Get them involved in something they can feel good about. Do something with them on a regular basis to show them that adults can be counted on. Help them see behind their current pain to a life full of future possibilities. There is hope ahead!

What happens when a young person comes to visit with you in your role as an adult leader and says, "I have a drinking problem"? How can you help?

- Be compassionate. Show them that you love and respect them as a child of God.
- Learn the facts about alcoholism.
- Understand your own emotions and reactions.
- Help them face the truth with themselves, with family members, and with other young people in the congregation.
- Continue to show support and love for the alcoholic and their family.
- Take *action*. Now that they have revealed their "problem," don't

let it be swept back under the rug. This may be a real chance for recovery. Point them to any number of resources available in your community (Alcoholics Anonymous and professional counseling among others).

- Make an appointment with them in a reasonable time so they may report to you what steps they've taken.
- Expect a long, involved treatment that will not solve all of the problems that the alcoholic or their family members have.

What if a young person comes to you and says, "My friend has a problem. How can I help?" Share the above ways to help, but at the same time make sure that you share these *don'ts*:

- Don't drink along with your friend, thinking you're consoling them or that you can slow the pace of their drinking. This only reinforces their habit.
- Don't give or loan them any money.
- Don't cover up the problem by lying for them in order to shield them from the consequences of their actions.
- Don't clean up after them (either their vomit or their trash).
- Don't take over their responsibilities. This can only diminish their self-worth.
- Don't make excuses for their behavior ("His parents are giving him a rough time." "Her boyfriend just broke up with her").
- Don't demand unrealistic promises, such as "I'll just quit right now forever." Don't let them make promises they can't keep.
- Don't try to reason with them when they're not sober.
- Don't ignore the situation.

Do encourage the young person to take care of *themselves* and not get drawn into the lifestyle of the alcoholic. The young person may want to join Al-Anon or Alateen, a voluntary program for those twelve to twenty years of age with alcoholic friends or relatives that provides friendship and information.

Teenage Pregnancy

Just the Facts

- In 1990, there were an estimated one million pregnancies and 521,626 births to U.S. women aged fifteen to nineteen years.[1]

- From 1980 to 1991, the number of births to women ten to fourteen years old rose from 1.1 per 1,000 women to 1.4 per 1,000 women. The number of births to women fifteen to nineteen years old rose from 53.0 to 62.1 per 1,000.[2]

- From 1950 to 1980, the number of live births to unmarried women aged fifteen to nineteen rose from 12.6 to 27.6 per 1,000 women. From 1980 to 1991, the number of births rose again to 44.8 per 1,000 women.[3]

- From 1973 to 1990 the percent of females between the ages of fifteen to nineteen who became pregnant increased from ten percent to 11.5 percent, and stayed level at 11.5 percent through 1991. Pregnancy is more prevalent among teens ages eighteen to nineteen than among teens ages fifteen to seventeen. National survey data indicates that 86 percent of pregnancies to teens under age twenty were unintended.[4]

- Between 1960 and 1985 teen birth rates fell from 89.1 to 51 births per 1,000. Between 1985 and 1991 the teen birth rate increased to 62.1 per 1,000, and between 1991 and 1993 the rates fell to 59.6 per 1,000.[5]

- The 1994 birth rate among teenagers aged fifteen to nineteen was five percent lower than the recent high of 62.1 in 1991. The decline from 1993 to 1994 in teenage births was one percent for teenagers aged fifteen to seventeen (to 37.6 per 1,000 women) and one percent for teenagers eighteen to nineteen years old (to 91.5 births per 1,000 women).[6]

- Recent declines in abortion rates and birth rates for teenagers indicate that the teenage pregnancy rate has also fallen in the 1990s.[7]

- Condoms have an eighteen percent failure rate among teenagers.[8]

- Every year, three million teens—about one in four sexually experienced teens—acquire an STD (sexually transmitted disease).[9]

- In a single act of unprotected sex with an infected partner, a teenage woman has a one percent risk of acquiring HIV, a thirty percent risk of getting genital herpes, and a fifty percent chance of contracting gonorrhea.[10]

- In 1995, the reported number of cases of chlamydia infection (477,638) exceeded the reported number of cases of gonorrhea (392,848) in the United States. In 1995, for every chlamydia case detected and reported in males, almost six cases were detected in females [because of screening strategies that focus on females].[11]

Overview of Teenage Pregnancy Solutions

Why can't we conquer the problem? The dilemma of how to stop or slow the rate of teenage pregnancy is complex. Many different perspectives can be argued and many friends and foes are drawn into the fray.

Certainly many folks point to the meteoric rise of episodes of sex acts in the movies and on television. This makes some believe that the battle line must be drawn facing the media. The solution for these advocates is to call for more responsible producers and directors who will at the same time decrease the number of sex acts, depict more responsible sexual behavior, and show the consequences of irresponsible behavior.

The struggle to reduce the number of teenage pregnancies is caught up in a battle between those who believe that social programs (many government funded) are the answer and those who believe that personal morality and virtue is the heart of the answer.

A focus on abstinence among young people would seem to be the best option statistically for lowering the rate of teenage pregnancy and the transmission of STDs. This draws fire from those who either believe that it is an unrealistic goal for the majority of today's young people, that it points the moral finger too harshly at those who have had sex even once, or that it has no impact at all on those who engage in frequent sex.

Teaching that sex before marriage is wrong is still a valued solution, but opponents once again point to a lack of religious foundation among many young people today that could make this solution more certain.

Teaching young women and young men to say no seems to be a more and more helpful solution to the dilemma. Many surveys of women of different ages and socioeconomic backgrounds all point to a high interest of young women in learning these skills. Along with these refusal skills often go programs that enhance self-confidence and self-esteem.

A focus on teen parenting in high schools seems to be part of a helpful solution. It has been said many times that having a young person take care of an infant for a full day is a cheap and effective method of birth control! What, however, of those young people who enjoy the experience?

A focus for teens to stop having sexual intercourse seems to be gathering support in some areas of the country. But this depends on identifying those who are currently having frequent sex and placing them into a targeted program. This is not an easy task and not one that could be used in a widespread way.

Program Design on Teenage Pregnancy

Before doing a program on teen pregnancy, it should be noted that such a program is dangerous. There may be some in your youth group who have had sex at least once, and there may even be some who are frequently having sex. There may even be one who has been pregnant and either carried the child to term (which you probably would have known about) or who had an abortion or miscarriage (which you may not have known about). The last thing you would want to do is to have a program that would make any young person feel alienated from the body of Christ that could instead offer them love and support.

There will certainly be some members of the congregation who will expect that if you do offer a program on teen pregnancy, you will speak forthrightly and openly and say to all who will listen: "The Bible and the church say that sex before marriage is wrong. Pregnancy and STDs are the result of sin and should be recognized as such."

There will be some members of your congregation who will take a softer view, many perhaps because they themselves had a child before marriage or are women who had an abortion (whether before marriage or during marriage). They may be active members of the congregation and may be unwilling to relive their situations. They may have had family members who were in these dilemmas. For whatever reasons, they will be more sympathetic to those caught in the predicament of teenage pregnancy and less willing to be judgmental or hard-line about such a matter.

So what are the options? The choice of most, sadly enough (including myself), is to say nothing, to have no programs either during church school or during an evening session that address this matter. It's too dangerous; it ought to be left in the hands of either individual families or the schools.

Another choice, more frequently chosen but still not the majority, would be to face the issue head-on and come down with a hard-line. But for reasons mentioned above, I don't prefer this option.

So what's left? Where is the solid ground in this matter—the arena where debate and discussion can take place; where young people can safely go home and share their experience at youth group and not be put on the "firing line"; where you won't be getting a number of angry phone calls the next day; and, by the way, a program that the young person will come to so that you won't be preaching to an empty house.

My suggestion: Focus on what many young people and adults are looking for—a relationship that is real and will last. So with fear and trepidation, here is a starter program design that will attempt to get at the teen pregnancy issue in a wiser and safer fashion.

Program Design for Educating about Teenage Relationships

Theme

Male–Female relationships—What are some building blocks to relationships that are real?

Objectives

By the end of the session, participants will be able to

- list five ways to enrich a relationship with someone of the opposite gender without having sex

- name one story from the Bible where a sexual relationship led to trouble

- name at least two building blocks of a lasting relationship

Materials Needed

- Wooden blocks
- Index cards, scissors, tape, markers
- Bibles

➡ Activity One ⬅

Get some wooden blocks from your congregation's church school room (be sure to put them back!) or borrow them from a family with a young child. Cut index cards to fit on one of the wide sides of the block and have tape ready to attach these cards to the blocks. Also have dark-color markers ready to write on the cards (before you tape them to the blocks so that the marker won't bleed through). As the group gathers, let them build with the blocks and have a good time.

After most of the group has gathered, pull out index cards and markers and ask the group to brainstorm ideas for building blocks for a lasting relationship with someone of the opposite gender. As they toss their ideas out, write each on a card and tape it to a block. Don't attempt to build a structure with any design, just lay them on a table or ledge of a chalkboard. Sex, honesty, trust, friendship, intimacy, love, and many more ought to come up. Get a young person to help you if you like. If this activity leads to some discussion, that's fine.

➡ Activity Two ⬅

At this point, change the tone of the discussion by asking

- As we consider these building blocks, what would TV and the movies want us to believe is one of the first steps in a lasting relationship with someone of the opposite gender?

Of course, the answer is sex. Ask them to name some TV shows and recent movies that indicate this, or better yet, ask them to name some TV shows or movies where a lasting relationship with someone of the opposite gender is not built primarily on sex! Everything we know—medically, morally, and biblically—tells us that sexual intercourse before the respect and commitment found in marriage is risky and dangerous. Ask the young people to give some examples (STDs, pregnancy, dropping out of school). Let's look at a couple of stories in the Bible where sexual intercourse gets people into trouble.

Hand out Bibles and ask the young people to look up the stories of Abraham and Hagar *(Gen. 16)* and David and Bathsheba *(2 Sam. 11).*

Continue by asking youth to not get the idea that sex is bad. It is good! God made us sexual beings and God created us good *(Gen. 1:31)*. But lasting, rich relationships are not built on sexual intercourse. Explain that often sex is a great threat to a relationship, especially before or outside of marriage. People in love show each other love in many other ways besides sexual intercourse. Challenge youth to build a new structure and see how many blocks they can stack with as many different ideas as possible.

What are ways that two people can show each other love other than through the act of sexual intercourse? Use these ideas as starters:

- hold hands

- talk on the phone

- write a poem

- watch a sunset

- eat dinner by candlelight

- dedicate a song on the radio

- share an ice cream cone

- do homework together

- go on a picnic

- respect each other

As each of these ideas pops up, especially if they are fast, dump the blocks on the floor in the middle of the room along with the tape, markers, and index cards and let everyone start writing, taping, and building. At some point either you'll run out of blocks or you'll run out of time.

Point out that you get to a lasting, rich relationship by many small, continued activities. You get to relationships built of honesty, trust, love, and, yes, sex, by first starting small and then, interestingly enough, by continuing small. You might fall in love, but it takes far more work than sex to *stay* in love.

➤➤ Activity Three ◀◀

As a way of closing and reminding everyone that grace and forgiveness are found in the Bible, encourage youth to look at a story with Jesus in it. Have participants turn to *John 8:1–11* and ask someone to read the passage aloud. Our faith is not one of condemnation, but one of love. Every person has the right to change their behavior and enjoy God's love and grace. Jesus cared for people and God wants the very best for us. Close with prayer giving thanks for our bodies created as good gifts from God.

Help for the Adult Leader

Well, we've skipped and danced around the whole issue of teenage pregnancy, so now it's time to answer the question "Is sex before marriage wrong?" My own personal answer is "yes," but in the very same breath I want to say that adult leaders of young people cannot afford to stop here with that answer. If they are to serve the young people that they minister to and with, they must also be open and ready to listen to those young people who made choices other than those we would want chosen. They must also be mindful of the mistakes that they themselves as humans make every day. We are all sinful and in need of God.

If we are loving, accepting, and open to young people, it should come as no surprise that someday a young person will reveal a serious matter, such as teen pregnancy, to us. So before we get into advice giving, it makes sense for you as an adult leader of young people to have a long heart-to-heart conversation over the matter of *confidentiality* with your colleagues in ministry—other adult leaders as well as church staff. Talk about the following:

- What are your state laws regarding confidentiality and disclosure?
- What matters and conversations with young people are legitimate for you as an adult leader to keep confidential?
- What matters and conversations between adult leaders and young people should be shared afterward with colleagues and /or church staff?
- Out of those that *must* be shared, which are matters that will probably be "taken out of the hands" of the adult leader because they are of such a serious nature?

The Peer Helping Class at Owen High School in Swannanoa, North Carolina, came up with these answers to the question "What are the exceptions to confidentiality?" (Again, check your state laws.)

- Suicide
- Abuse
- Sexual harassment
- Possession of drugs or weapons

Whatever answers your youth ministry team comes up with, I believe that these guidelines should be flexible and may change over time. But it's clear that your conversations about confidentiality must indeed take place with your colleagues, both volunteer and paid, and the sooner the better.

That way, when the fateful time comes that a young person (either male or female) sits down with you and reveals a teen pregnancy, you'll know what the confidentiality guidelines are and will be on a firm footing with the young person. You will be able to tell the young person what you will and will not reveal and who you are obligated to reveal it to. Although the potential of revealing it to a wider audience may be upsetting to the young person, they almost surely will have considered this possibility before coming to you and will have still found it important to come and talk to *you*.

Whether you as an adult leader are talking to a young person or the family of the young person, the response should be basically the same:

• Let's not play the blame game.

• You are a child of God, and God loves you.

• We (the church, the adult leaders, etc.) love you.

• We all are human and therefore make mistakes . . . both you and we.

• There is no mistake that we can't get through together and with God's help.

So, then, the response of the adult leader is one of compassion—not advice, not rescue, not "passing the buck," but compassion.

When the Shock Comes: Working Through Traumatic Events with Young People

Sooner or later it's going to happen. You've heard all of the stories, and perhaps even lived through some of them. You tried to imagine what you as an adult leader would have done if it had been *your* youth group when

- one of the members attempted suicide
- a friend of many of the young people completed suicide
- a church staff person was arrested on charges of sexual abuse
- a youth hayride turned tragic when the tractor turned over and killed the driver
- a young person drowned while on a church-sponsored whitewater rafting trip
- multiple drug arrests were made at the local high school in one day
- parent of a young person was killed suddenly in a car accident
- the church van rolled over on a trip through the mountains and, even though no one was killed, there were multiple injuries

They are horrible possibilities to imagine. Here are some guidelines for a process of dealing with a group of young people as they process a traumatic or stressful event. Before calling a gathering:

- Find a "safe" setting (hopefully at the church) for both the young people and the adults leading the meeting.
- Secure at least two adults to "run process," hopefully one of them a pastor.
- Determine, with the help of the other adult leaders, whether any helping professional or other outside adults ought to be invited to the meeting.
- As invitations to the gathering go out, make sure that the young people know what adult leaders will be there and if any helping professionals will be in attendance (so there won't be any surprises). This will also give parents some confidence in your meeting.

Make sure that everyone is clear on the purpose of the gathering: The meeting is designed to help persons who have experienced a traumatic event process the experience with others involved in the same event. The great stress felt now will probably lessen in time, but this gathering will help the young people get their feelings out, deal with the situation in an honest way, and reduce their stress *more quickly*. Talking is good. It also helps an individual see that others have many of their same feelings and that they are not alone. There is more help available. The pieces of the puzzle can be put together to form a whole picture of the event that will be helpful to all.

Write the ground rules on newsprint or a chalkboard for the group to see as they come in.

Ground Rules for a Gathering to Deal with Tragedy

- You don't have to say anything.
- Speak only for yourself and not for others.
- What is said in this room stays in this room.
- This is *not* an investigation into what happened.
- Don't criticize others (in this gathering or absent from the gathering).
- You are expected to stay the entire meeting even though you may decide not to participate. It may be difficult.

When the meeting starts, follow these ten steps in order

1. Go over the purpose of the meeting again.

2. Go over the posted ground rules for all and get agreement or ask those who won't agree to leave.

3. Go around the room and let everyone introduce themselves if they don't know each other (especially the adults).

4. Tell participants that they will move through four steps in this meeting: What did you see? What were you thinking? What reactions/feelings do you have to the event? What have we learned? Then the gathering will be closed with prayer.

5. Begin the step "What did you see?" This assumes that there are people in the room who were actual observers. If not, this may move into "What did you hear happened?"

6. Move into the step "What were you thinking as the event

Dealing with Crisis

happened?" Again, this assumes that there are participants in the room who were actually there. Otherwise the discussion moves directly to step 7.

7. "What was your immediate reaction?" It may take a while to get into feelings, but it will happen! "What additional feelings have you had since then, now that this has had time to sink in?"

8. "What can we learn about what feelings are happening to us now and what feelings we may have in the future?" This is the time to talk in a more general way about the emotions that the young people and their friends are having and may have in the future and how to deal with them.

9. I Identify resources (people, organizations, and books) forever one's continuing use in the times to come.

10. Close with prayer.

Dos for the Adult Leader

- Be calm.
- Actively listen.
- Help clarify what others are saying.
- Help participants understand that what they are feeling is normal.
- Use body language to indicate your interest.
- Use eye contact to show the young people that they have your full attention.
- Help the young people explore their fears.
- Do all this and talk as little as possible.

Don'ts for the Adult Leader

- Don't tell them that "everything will be all right."
- Don't judge participants by the way they feel or act.
- Don't let your own emotions get out of control. Be a good model by showing appropriate emotion.
- Don't try to figure out whose "fault" it was.
- Don't try to give participants more information than they need.
- Don't give up being the group leader. They need your guidance.

Close your gathering with prayer. Perhaps you might use a prayer of affirmation by having each participant offer a sentence of thanksgiving for a gift the person on his or her left brings to the world and to the group.

The Next Step?

There's a movement sweeping the country—or maybe it's just my wishful thinking that there ought to be a movement sweeping the country. What would happen if every church youth group became determined to teach the skills of dealing with the crises of life? This would involve young people before they needed those skills. Of course, that's not possible—we've all been involved in the crises of life already. But just because we've struggled through them, can't we learn new skills for dealing with them? And wouldn't youth feel more confident when a crisis hit if they not only had picked up the needed skills and knew an adult leader that they could turn to, but also had a peer group that they knew had learned the same skills and would understand what they were going through, would know how to empathize with them in the best way, and might be able to coach them through the crisis? Better yet, what if youth knew someone to intervene in their struggle to deal with a crisis in an effort to put them on the right track?

Now admittedly, not all of our young people would be interested in learning those skills, but wouldn't it be better to expect them to? Not all of our young people will be involved personally with every crisis that we taught them the skills for dealing with, but won't they at some point in their life? Not all will help another friend/peer, but shouldn't it be expected of them to reach out? Not all will practice those skills, not all will attempt to use those skills in a crisis, but isn't it appropriate that the church help nurture skills for helping someone in crisis? Imagine with me: What would happen?

The Appendix of this book lists resources for information and assistance to help in developing these skills.

Appendix
Resources for Information and Assistance

Alcohol Abuse

Alcoholics Anonymous
General Service Office
PO Box 459
Grand Central Station
New York, NY 10163
(212) 870-3400

American Council for Drug Education
(ACDE)
164 W. 74th St.
New York, NY 10023
1-800-488-DRUG

National Clearinghouse for
Alcohol and Drug Information
PO Box 2345
Rockville, MD 20847-2345
1-800-729-6686 or
(301) 468-2600

National Federation of Parents
for Drug Free Youth
8730 Georgia Avenue
Suite 200
Silver Springs, MD 20910
(301) 585-6118

Parent Resources and Information for
Drug Education (PRIDE)
3610 DeKalb Technology Pkwy.
Suite 105
Atlanta, GA 30340
(770) 458-9900

General

Centers for Disease Control and
Prevention (CDC)
1600 Clifton Rd. NE
Atlanta, GA 30333
(404) 639-3534
Fax Information Service:
(404) 332-4565

Clearinghouse on Health Indexes
Division of Analysis
National Center for Health Statistics
6525 Belcrest Road
Hyattsvville, MD 20782
(301) 436-7035

Consumer Information Center
PO Box 100
Pueblo, CO 81002

Health Reports

U.S. General Accounting Office (GAO)
PO Box 6015
Gaithersburg, MD 20884
(202) 512-6000
internet: www.gao.gov

National Institutes of Health
9000 Rockville Pike
Bethesda, MD 20892
(301) 443-4536

Office of Disease Prevention
and Health Promotion
National Health Information Center
PO Box 1133
Washington, DC 20013
(301) 565-4167
http://nhic-nt.health.org
e-mail: nhicinfo@health.org

Surgeon General
Parklawn Bldg. #18-66
5600 Fishers Lane
Rockville, MD 20857

Diagnostic and Statistical Manual of Mental Disorders: DSM-IV. 4th ed. Washington, DC: American Psychiatric Association, 1994.

Suicide

American Association of Suicidology
(AAS) publishes a professional journal,
Suicide and Life-Threatening Behavior, and
sponsors an annual conference to provide
a forum for the presentation of recent
research activities and current suicide
prevention programs:

American Association of Suicidology
4201 Connecticut Avenue, NW
Suite 310
Washington, DC 20008

Suicide: Let's Talk About It, a youth course
and professionally produced video,
available for $8.75 from Presbyterian
Distribution Service at 1-800-524-2612,
Item #04281. "Teacher's Aide," a
Presbyterian Church (U.S.A.) publication,
comments that it was viewed by a group
of adults ranging in age from twenty to

sixty and all found it very valuable. It deals honestly with teen suicide. *Suicide*, a free brochure, is also available from PDS at 1-800-524-2612.

Teenage Pregnancy

Center for Population Research
Contraception Evaluation Branch
6100 Executive Blvd. Room 8B07
Bethesda, MD 20892
(301) 496-4924

National Maternal and Child Health Clearinghouse
2070 Chain Bridge Rd.
Vienna, VA 22182
(703) 821-8955

Office of Adolescent Pregnancy Programs
U.S. Department of Health and Human Services
4350 East West Hwy, Suite 200
Bethesda, MD 20814
(301) 594-4004

Planned Parenthood Federation of America's Katharine Dexter McCormick Library
810 Seventh Avenue,
New York, NY
(212) 261-4637
e-mail: communications@ppfa.org

Encyclopedia

First, a disclaimer. The purpose of this "encyclopedia" is to give the adult leader of youth a ready reference and to encourage us all to begin thinking of possible responses when a crisis hits. A "quick and dirty" index of this kind cannot even come close to the assistance and experience that a helping professional might provide. I hope that you'll begin collecting articles for your own files and books that you think might be helpful in the future.

Alcohol Abuse of Friends

- Issues: My friend is losing control and changing into a different person. How can I help?
- Your Best Response: "There are some ways that you can help, but there are things that you need to avoid doing as well. Let's talk."

Anorexia Nervosa

- Issues: intense fear of being fat or gaining weight. Refuses to maintain a normal weight.
- Your Best Response: "Let's go talk to your family right now. We need to set up an appointment for you to see a professional like your family doctor."

Arrest of Member of Family of Young Person

- Issues: fear, shame, confusion.
- Your Best Response: "We're here to support you through this time of crisis in the life of your family."

Arrest of Member of Church Staff

- Issues: betrayal, confusion, shock, denial.
- Your Best Response: "We'll let the legal system handle anything that has been

done that was wrong. But it's the church's job to show God's love and care to both the accused and the victim(s)."

Arrest of Friend of Young Person

- Issues: Denial, guilt (I could have done something).
- Your Best Response: "We'll let the legal system handle anything that has been done that was wrong. But it's the church's job to show God's love and care to both the accused and the victim(s)."

Bulimia Nervosa

- Issues: fear of gaining weight; binge eating of large quantities followed by purging.
- Your Best Response: "Let's go talk to your family. We need to get you an appointment to see a professional."

"Coming Out"

- Issues: What will people think of me now that my friend has revealed he or she is gay or lesbian?
- Your Best Response: "Your friend has decided that they could no

longer live a lie. You have to live your life without worrying about what other people will think."

Death (Sudden Accident)

- Issues: This can't be happening. Why did God let this happen?
- Your Best Response: "It is real and we'll help you deal with it. God loved _____ and loves you. It's OK to be angry."

Depression

- Issues: can't seem to see the light at the end of the tunnel. No energy.
- Your Best Response: Accept the current depression. If you determine that the depression is continuing or worsening, refer immediately to a helping professional.

When Disaster Strikes

- Issues: Why is this happening to me/us?
- Your Best Response: Dig in immediately and find some help so that there can be some positive response quickly. We are humans and our world is governed by natural laws.

Divorce of Parents of Young Person

- Issues: What did I do wrong? Why did they do this to me?
- Your Best Response: "Your parents have decided that they can no longer live together. That is not your fault. Your task now is how to love each of them separately."

HIV Positive

- Issues: fear for own health, grief for friend, concern over what others will think
- Your Best Response: "You have a chance to learn more about both life and death as you support your friend during their illness. Let's talk."

Illness (Critical) of Young Person

- Issues: Will I die? Why is this happening to me? What did I do wrong?
- Your Best Response: "No matter what happens, we're here for you and will care for you and your family. God loves you."

Illness (Terminal) of Family Member of Young Person

- Issues: What will happen to me after they die? Why can't I just live my life like a normal teenager without having to deal with this?
- Your Best Response: "We're here to care for you and your family when death comes to your loved one. And we're here to help you learn from this experience."

Moving, Best Friend

- Issues: loss, grief, fear that they will never have another friend like this one.
- Your Best Response: "It's almost like someone died. It will take you a while to get over this, won't it?"

Pregnancy

- Issues: shame over mistake, worry over what others will think, fear of rejection by friends.
- Your Best Response: "We're here to show our love and God's love for you and for your child. We'll help you through this. It is a crisis that is temporary, not permanent.

Suicide Attempted

- Issues: desperate cry for help.
- Your Best Response: "Let's talk...and talk...and talk some more. There is hope."

Suicide Completed

- Issues: tragic loss, guilt over inability to "save" their friend/loved one.
- Your Best Response: "This will be hard to get through, but with God's help we will get through it. This was your friend's decision. I'm sorry that they didn't realize that there were so many other options."

Notes

1. Survivors of a Completed Suicide

1. "The mind in its despair," *U.S. News & World Report*, Aug. 9, 1993, p. 34.

2. "U.S. Injury Mortality Statistics," from the latest site of the Center for Disease Control and Prevention, http://www.cdc.gov.

3. "Death with Honors: Suicide Among Gifted Adolescents," by James R. Delisle, in *Journal of Counseling and Development*, Vol. 64 May 1986, p. 560.

4. "The mind in its despair," *U.S. News & World Report*, p. 34.

5. "The mind in its despair," *U.S. News & World Report*, p. 34.

6. "U.S. Injury Mortality Statistics."

7. Ibid.

8. "The mind in its despair," *U.S. News & World Report*, p. 34.

2. Attempted Suicide

1. "Youth and Suicide," by the Rev. Joyce Ann Mercer, in *Alert,* vol. 26, no. 2 (August 1996), p. 7.

2. "Death with Honors: Suicide Among Gifted Adolescents," by James R. Delisle, in *Journal of Counseling and Development*, vol. 64 (May 1986), p. 560.

3. Hermann Hesse, *Steppenwolf* (New York, NY: Bantam, 1975), p. 55.

4. "Youth and Suicide," in *Alert,* pp. 7–9.

5. "Responding to Adolescent Suicide," by Sidney Barish, in *Education Digest,* January 1992, p. 62.

3. Alcohol Abuse

1. World Wide Web page of Mothers Against Drunk Driving (MADD), http://www.gran-net.com/madd, Dec. 28, 1996.

2. Ibid.

3. Ibid.

4. Ibid.

5. "1995 National Household Survey on Drug Abuse," on the World Wide Web page of the National Clearinghouse for Alcohol and Drug Information, http://www.health.org, Dec. 28, 1996.

6. Ibid.

7. Ibid.

8. Ibid.

9. Ibid.

10. Ibid.

11. "NCADD Fact Sheet: Youth and Alcohol," from the National Council on Alcoholism and Drug Dependence, June 1990.

12. Ibid.

13. Ibid.

14. "Alcoholism Runs in Families," on the World Wide Web page of the National Clearinghouse for Alcohol and Drug Information, http://www.health.org, Dec. 28, 1996.

15. Ibid.

4. Teenage Pregnancy

1. "MMWR Weekly Report—Preview," Monthly Morbidity Weekly Report, October 1, 1993, vol. 42, no. 38. From the Internet site of the Centers for Disease Control and Prevention, http://www.cdc.gov.

2. "Youth Indicators, 1996: Trends in the Well-Being of American Youth," by Thomas D. Snyder and Linda L. Shafer, published on the Internet site of the National Center for Education Statistics, http://www.ed.gov/NCES.

3. Ibid.

4. "Profile of America's Youth," from the Internet site of the U.S. Department of Health and Human Services, http://youth.os.dhhs.gov/youthinf.htm.

5. Ibid.

6. "Teenage Births Drop for Third Straight Year," published on the Internet site of the Centers for Disease Control and Prevention, http://www.cdc.gov, June 24, 1996.

7. Ibid.

8. "Condoms and Contraceptives in Junior High and High School Clinics: What Do You Think?" by Glen C. Griffin, MD, in *Postgraduate Medicine*, April 1993, pp. 1–4.

9. "Teen Sex and Pregnancy," from Facts in Brief, The Alan Guttmacher Institute, August 1996.

10. Ibid.

11. "Sexually Transmitted Disease Surveillance 1995," published on the Internet site of the Centers for Disease Control and Prevention, http://www.cdc.gov, September 1996.